# I know
# I came
# in here
# for
# something...

Lighthearted devotions
and chuckles for
embracing those
Senior Moments

*Inspired
by Faith*

I know I came in here for something...
ISBN 978-0-9853005-6-2

Published by Product Concept Mfg., Inc.
2175 N. Academy Circle #200, Colorado Springs, CO 80909

Written and Compiled by Patricia Mitchell
in association with Product Concept Mfg., Inc.

All scripture quotations are from the King James version
of the Bible unless otherwise noted.

Scriptures taken from the Holy Bible,
New International Version®, NIV®.
Copyright © 1973, 1978, 1984 by Biblica, Inc.™
Used by permission of Zondervan.
All rights reserved worldwide.
www.zondervan.com

Sayings not having a credit listed are contributed by writers
for Product Concept Mfg., Inc. or in a rare case,
the author is unknown.

I know
I came
in here
for
something...

I'd like to grow very old as slowly as possible.
Charles Lamb

*You came in here for something…
now what was it? Don't worry.
You'll think of it as soon as you
leave the room!*

Yes, those "senior moments" happen, so
what better time than now to put up a fight?
No, it doesn't include a time machine (you
wouldn't really want to be 18 again, would
you?), but it does include some exercise.
For your funny bone, that is.

This is a collection of upbeat reflections,
timeless truths, and just-for-fun smiles designed
to whet your wit and tickle your fancy, because,
after all, those senior moments are pretty funny.
And there's no age limit on laughter. In fact,
that's something that gets better and better!

Grow old with me!
The best is yet to be.
Robert Browning

5

"Judging by my
LAUGH LINES,
you'd think my life's
been a RIOT."

# It's a Gift

It seems only yesterday you would hold up four fingers and make sure your grandma knew you weren't four, but four and a half! Then you spent a good part of your teens trying—praying!—to look older than your tender years, and now...well, now you don't want to think about age at all.

But do think about it. Think about the blessing of being here this day...of having done, seen, and experienced so much...of the memories you wouldn't trade for anything...of being who you are, where you are.

Let us be glad and rejoice.
Revelation 19:7

Concerned about a neighbor she hasn't seen in a few days, Mom tells her young son to go over and ask how old Mrs. Smith is doing. He does so, and comes back in five minutes.

"How is she?" says Mom.

"Fine, but she's sure mad at you," her son replies.

"Mad at me? Why in the world would she be mad at me?"

"Because," the boy explains, "Mrs. Smith says it's none of your business how old she is!"

I'm not 50—
I'm 35 with 15 years' experience.

We don't stop playing because we
grow old; we grow old because we
stop playing.
George Bernard Shaw

To remain young while growing old
is the highest blessing.
Proverb

## It might be a question of age if…

- The candles on your last birthday cake significantly contributed to global warming.

- You're more interested in how long your car will last rather than how fast it will go.

- You feel you've finally got your head together, but now your body is falling apart.

- You don't bother to suck in your stomach, no matter who walks into the room.

A little girl was sitting with her mother watching TV when she turned to her mom and asked, "Mommy, how come there's so much gray in your hair?"

Hoping to make this a teachable moment, Mom replied, "Because every time you disobey me, I get another gray hair."

After a few minutes, the girl turned to her mother again. "Then how come Grandma's hair is all gray?"

A woman was called to testify in court. "What's your age, ma'am?" the attorney asked. "And let me remind you, you're under oath."

"I'm 39 and some months," she said hesitantly.

"Just how many months?" the attorney pressed.

In a voice barely above a whisper, she replied, "about 240."

At a gathering, an older woman thought she'd have some fun by asking a young man to guess her age. When he hesitated, she said, "You must have some idea how old I am."

"Yes, I do," the young man replied with a smile. "But I can't decide whether to make it ten years younger because of your appearance, or ten years older because of your intelligence."

It's IMPORTANT
to leave a
TWINKLE
in your
WRINKLES!

# Might as Well Laugh

Ever sat down in a restaurant next to a table full of seniors? Ever gotten together with a few longtime friends? More often than not, everyone was cracking jokes, telling stories, and laughing—heads-back, hands-on-the-belly laughing.

At a certain age, we finally hit the point where we realize that really fantastic times can cost no more than the price of a cup of coffee. Times like this simply need our stubborn refusal to let anything come between us and another great day.

Rejoice in the Lord always:
and again I say, Rejoice.
Philippians 4:4

Life is short—
Stretch out the good times.

None are so old as those who have
outlived enthusiasm.
Henry David Thoreau

It's not what we have, but what we
enjoy, that constitutes our abundance.
Epicurus

# How to have a great day:

1. Open a document on your computer.

2. Title the document My Problems.

3. List your problems, and then close the document.

4. Now send the document My Problems to the Recycle Bin.

5. When the computer asks you, "Are you sure you want to delete My Problems permanently?" press Yes.

6. Feel happier?

With every new gray hair, dear God,
Please bless me with a smile—
I've wrinkles and a midriff bulge,
So help me walk with style.

Dear God, whatever years may bring,
There's one thing that I pray—
Grant me a joyful attitude
And laughter every day!

Five longtime friends were sitting at a table in a café. Over lunch, one complained about her recalcitrant teenagers, another about her husband. A third roundly criticized her boss, and a fourth friend launched into a detailed description of her recent surgery. The fifth regaled her friends with all that went wrong at her house over the weekend.

After listening, the waiter came to the table and asked, "Is *anything* okay?"

Laugh, and the world laughs
with you. Cry, and you have to
blow your nose.

The older you get, the fewer
things you're willing to waste
time worrying about.

When grace is joined with wrinkles,
it is adorable.
Victor Hugo

AGE is an issue
of MIND
over MATTER.
If YOU don't MIND,
it doesn't
MATTER.

*Mark Twain*

# What If?

Suppose you tell Age what's up. It's standing there tapping its feet and awaiting instructions, so you'd better start barking some orders now. You sure don't want Age telling you what to do!

Start now. Here are a few ideas for starters. Say:

"Age, throw away all those negative feelings and stereotypes littering my head. And I don't mean recycle them—get rid of them!"

"And then, you know what? Get out of my way—I've got things I wanna do!"

Every tree is known
by his own fruit.
Luke 6:44

What if you slept?
And what if, in your sleep, you dreamed?
And what if, in your dream, you went to heaven
and there plucked a strange and beautiful flower?
And what if, when you awoke,
you had the flower in your hand?
Ah, what then?

Samuel Taylor Coleridge

As one grows older, one climbs
with surprising strides.
George Sand

I speak the truth not so much as I
would, but as much as I dare, and I
dare a little more as I grow older.
Michel de Montaigne

Don't let your age get you down—
it's too hard to get back up again.

Age is all in your head. But anyone
with bifocals, tooth implants,
cataract surgery, and gray hair is
well aware of that.

Youth belongs to those who
still believe in the beauty of
their dreams.

Get action. Seize the moment.
Man was never intended to become
an oyster.
Theodore Roosevelt

Few people know how to be old.
François de la Rouchefoucauld

There comes a time in life when
we go into the attic and dust off
our dreams. Then we either polish
them up, or discard them out at
the curb.

She's found the secret of eternal
youth. She lies about her age.

# What if…

- You never tell yourself you're too old to start…
  or to give it a try?

- You refuse to accept stereotypes…
  not about others, and not about yourself?

- You think, speak, and act on the outside
  as young as you feel on the inside?

- You smile, laugh, and enjoy life for no other reason than because you can?

- You take advantage of being the age you are... because you can?

- You make dreams come true for yourself... and even for others? Because you can.

  And if not now, when?

EXPERIENCE
is what YOU got
by NOT having it
WHEN you
NEEDED IT.

# You Are Here

Most things get easier with experience, but it's not necessarily true about life. Or is it? Yes, there are troubles galore, some the same ones we've always known, but others we're just now having to cope with. That's hard!

What makes it a little easier is knowing that even troublesome things have a way of turning out okay. It's happened. You've experienced it. You've found that God has gotten you this far, and it's not likely He's going to let go of you now!

He is not far from each one of us.
Acts 17:27 NIV

The school of hard knocks is one
of those elite schools where each
student gets individual instruction.

I know God will not give me
anything I can't handle. I just wish
that He didn't trust me so much.

Mother Teresa

A proverb is no proverb to you
till life has illustrated it.

John Keats

Is your cucumber bitter? Throw it
away. Are there briars in your path?
Turn aside. That is enough. Do not
go on to say, "Why were things of
this sort ever brought into this world?"
Marcus Aurelius

Life would be infinitely happier if we
could only be born at the age of eighty
and gradually approach eighteen.
Mark Twain

A parachutist jumped from a plane, only to discover that his chute was broken. Plunging to the ground, he saw another man on the way up. "Hey," he yelled frantically to the man, "do you know anything about parachutes?"

"No," shouted the man. "Do you know anything about gas grills?"

The best thing one can do when
it's raining is to let it rain.
Henry Wadsworth Longfellow

Experience allows us to make new
mistakes instead of the old ones.

It just wouldn't be a picnic without
the ants.

We're only young once. After that, we have to come up with another excuse.

You know you're getting older when the current vintage look includes items of clothing you still have hanging in your closet.

Smooth seas do not make skillful sailors.

Two neighbors were locked in an on-going feud, and finally decided to take their case to court. When their day came, both appeared in front of the judge, arguing about who would go first with her side of the story. "All right," said the judge. "I'll hear the oldest person first."

The case was dismissed for lack of testimony.

IT usually takes
more than THREE
WEEKS to prepare
a good IMPROMPTU
SPEECH.

*Mark Twain*

# Speak Up

Have you ever filled out one of those surveys they send you after you've bought something? The choices offered don't tell half the story. Why, if they really wanted honest feedback, there'd be several options beyond "very satisfied" and "very dissatisfied."

For instance, how about "mildly annoying" and "downright exasperating" to cover loud music, condescending clerks, safety caps, bubble wrap, and blister-packs?

Do you think they'd listen? Probably not, but if God gave you a voice, it would be a shame not to use it.

A word spoken in due season,
how good is it!
Proverbs 15:23

# You know you're getting older when…

- All you exercise is your opinion.

- Store clerks give you the senior discount without you needing to ask for it.

- You find your all-time favorite music in the bargain bin.

- You examine every product and say, "They're just not making things like they used to."

A customer service rep wanted to make a mid-life career change, so he quit his job and joined the police force. After he had worked several months on the force, a friend asked him if he had any regrets.

"It's true, the hours are long and the work can be dangerous," the rookie officer reported, "but the thing I like about this job is that the customer is always wrong!"

It takes me a long time to lose my
temper, but once lost I could not find
it with a dog.
Mark Twain

Many a shopper's complaint is one of
long standing.

When the plane you are on is late, the
plane you want to transfer to is on time.

Everything is funny as long as it is
happening to somebody else.
Will Rogers

After Mom lectured her son on anger management, the boy asked, "But what's the difference between my uncontrolled anger and your frayed nerves?"

It's always good to remember that kisses are sweeter than whine.

Temper gets you into trouble. Pride keeps you there.

In the grocery check-out line, an older woman was standing in front of a young man. She turned and stared at him. He noticed, but tried to ignore her. After a few minutes, she said, "Young man, I'm sorry if my staring is making you uncomfortable, but you so remind me of my son. I haven't seen him in such a long time."

The young man smiled indulgently. "Oh, that's perfectly all right. Is there anything I can do for you?"

"Well, yes," the woman replied. "Would you—just as I'm leaving the cashier— say, 'Bye, Mom'?"

"Sure, I'm happy to do that."

So just as she was leaving, he waved and said cheerily, "Bye, Mom!"

Then when his order was rung up, the total came to $145. "That's impossible!" the man protested. "All I'm buying is some bread, milk and cereal!"

"Your mom said you'd pay for her," the cashier replied.

LIFE must
go on;
I FORGET
just WHY.

*Edna St. Vincent Millay*

# Right the First Time

The first time you open the refrigerator when you meant to open the cupboard, you laugh and tell a friend. But when you realize you've stored the ice cream in the oven, you're not laughing... and not telling. In fact, you pray no one else will notice the telltale drips.

Hey, you were right the first time. Laugh—and tell. It will make you feel better, and your friends, too. It'll encourage them to tell you about the time they put the ice cream in the dryer—and turned it on.

He that is of a merry heart
hath a continual feast.
Proverbs 15:15

An older driver pulled over to the side of the road when she heard the police car's siren. The officer walked up to her window and asked, "Now how long have you been driving without taillights?"

"Oh, no!" the woman screamed and jumped out of her car.

"Lady," the officer said, "calm down! It isn't that serious of an offense!"

"Well, just wait until my husband finds out!" she shouted.

The officer asked, "Where is he?"

"In the trailer that was hitched to the car!"

A woman began to notice a certain absent-mindedness in her longtime friend. "Do you often lose your train of thought?" she asked.

"Oh, not really," the friend replied, "but I have to admit that a few cars derail occasionally."

My computer started having memory problems, and I think it gave them to me.

An older patient went to see his physician. "I can't seem to remember anything anymore, Doc!"

"How long has this been going on?" the physician asked.

"How long has what been going on?"

May you never forget what is worth
remembering, nor ever remember
what is best forgotten.
Blessing

Why can we remember the tiniest
detail that has happened to us, and not
remember how many times we have
told it to the same person?
François de la Rochefoucauld

It is sometimes expedient to forget even
what you know.
Publilius Syrus

## It might be a question of age if…

- A package arrives from your favorite e-tailer, and you have to open it to find out what in the world it was that you ordered.

- You can wrap your own Christmas presents... and still be completely surprised when it comes time to open them!

- Someone walks up to you and says, "I'll bet you don't remember me!"—and they're absolutely right.

- You go to the doctor about your memory loss, and he asks you to pay your bill in advance.

- You make a list of things you want to do, and then can't remember where you put the list.

- You pause in the middle of a stairway to catch your breath, but then forget whether you were headed up or down.

- Life is full of wonder—you wonder where you parked the car...wonder if you dropped off the dry cleaning...wonder if you've picked it up yet...

We TURN no OLDER with years, but NEWER every DAY.

*Emily Dickinson*

# The Good Old Days

If we heard a toddler start to say "I remember the days...," we'd smile. Exactly how many days are we talking about here? But when anyone over 40 mutters similar words, we know we're in for a lament about how times have changed (they have a way of doing that) and how things just aren't what they used to be (never were).

The next time we mournfully start "remembering when," picture God smiling. Even if we think we're older than dirt, He's older. Way older. So we may as well smile, too.

From everlasting to everlasting, thou art God.
Psalm 90:2

The old begin to complain of the conduct of the young when they themselves are no longer able to set a bad example.

François de la Rochefoucauld

Enjoy yourself. These are the good old days you're going to miss in the years ahead.

Regret is an appalling waste of energy; you can't build on it; it's only for wallowing in.

Katherine Mansfield

A dad, frustrated at his teenager's highjinks, complained to a friend. "When I was his age, my dad sent me to my room. But my son's room is equipped with a high-speed computer, wi-fi, a color television, and state-of-the-art sound system!"

"So what do you do?" his friend asked.

"I send him to my room," the father replied.

## Remember when…

- Milk, eggs and sunshine were considered good for you?

- The only keyboard you owned was on the piano?

- More people counted their blessings instead of calories?

- The only web you knew about was the one hanging from your basement ceiling?

Though the man was getting on in years, he prided himself on his fitness and youthful appearance. His self-estimation was heightened one day when a sweet young woman sat down next to him on a plane that had no seat assignments, and plenty of other seats were available. She smiled, and the two of them fell into a delightful conversation.

After the plane landed and stopped at the gate, the woman unfastened her seat belt, stood up, and turned to her fellow passenger. "It was wonderful to talk to you," she said. "You remind me so much of my dad."

In the old days when people invented
a new function, they had something
useful in mind.

Henri Poincare

I like the dreams of the future better
than the history of the past.

Thomas Jefferson

When I was younger I could remember
anything, whether it happened or not.

Mark Twain

With the past, I have nothing to do;
nor with the future. I live now.

Ralph Waldo Emerson

I've NEVER
 seen a SMILING
 FACE that
was NOT
 beautiful.

# Not a Smoothie Anymore

The soft glowing face on the cover of almost any glossy magazine tells you more than you want to know. Sure, it's another boost to our youth culture, but before you sigh because that skin's not yours anymore, consider this—

That flawless complexion hasn't cried as much as you, but hasn't laughed as much, either. Those crow's-feet-free eyes don't reflect a lifetime of seeing and thinking and dreaming. That unlined mouth hasn't had the chance yet to comfort, encourage, guide, support.

And say "I love you" ...knowing what it really means to love.

God is love.
1 John 4:8

Every person is responsible for his
own looks after 40.

Abraham Lincoln

Never frown, for you never know
who is falling in love with your smile.

Beware, so long as you live, of judging
men by their outward appearance.

Jean de La Fontaine

Two 50-year-old women had lived on a farm all their lives, and they decided it was high time they go into the city and see the sights. Awed at one of the towering office buildings, they walked in the lobby and found themselves facing a set of metal doors. Just then the doors opened and an old lady walked in. A few minutes later, the doors opened again, and a young woman walked out.

The farm women look at each other, dumbstruck. "Next time those doors open," said one, "I'm gettin' in that thing!"

So much has been said and sung
of beautiful young girls, why doesn't
somebody wake up to the beauty of
old women?

Harriet Beecher Stowe

I don't mind getting older—it's the
maintenance that's getting me down.

Wrinkles should merely indicate where
smiles have been.

Mark Twain

In the grocery check-out line, a woman couldn't help but notice that the man in front of her had envelopes and stamps plastered in a symmetrical design all over his head. Curious, she tapped him on the shoulder and asked, "I hope I'm not being too nosy, but why do you have envelopes and stamps stuck all over your head?"

"Oh," the man replied, "it's my mail pattern baldness."

Time may be a great healer,
but it's a lousy beautician.

Beautiful young people are accidents
of nature, but beautiful old people
are works of art.
Eleanor Roosevelt

When the unqualified man started
working as a cosmetic surgeon, you'd
better believe it raised a few eyebrows.

With age comes the inner, the higher
life. Who would be forever young,
to dwell always in externals?
Elizabeth Cady Stanton

A little girl watched as her mother applied cold cream all over her face. "Why are you doing that?" the girl inquired.

"To make myself beautiful," Mom replied. Then she put the cap back on the jar of cold cream, pulled out a tissue, and began to wipe the cream off her face.

"What's the matter, Mommy?" the girl asked, "Are you giving up already?"

It's ALL
that the YOUNG
can DO for the
OLD, to SHOCK them
and KEEP them
UP to DATE.

*George Bernard Shaw*

# Life Out of the Loop

You know *the look*. It's the same one you gave your parents when they found the chart-topping, #1 hit song incomprehensible...and said so. How can you talk to people who are so out of the loop?

But now you're not only out of the loop, you're wondering exactly where the loop is anymore. By a certain point, you'll stop searching for that elusive sense of being oh-so-connected, give the loop the look, and be blessedly loop-less...or maybe just plain loopy.

I have learned,
in whatsoever state I am,
therewith to be content.
Philippians 4:11

There's nothing wrong with today's teenager that twenty years won't cure.

Teenagers have time and energy, but no money. Middle-agers have money and energy, but no time. Oldsters have time and money, but no energy.

I live to see the look on my grandkids' faces when I tell them that I'm older than the Internet.

"Jen and I want to get married," John told his friend, Jack. "Trouble is, we can't afford an apartment."

"Why don't you move in with Jen's parents?" asked Jack.

"There's no room," said John glumly, "because they're living with their parents."

The young are always ready to give
to those who are older than themselves
the full benefits of their inexperience.
Oscar Wilde

You can tell that a child is growing up
when she stops asking where she came
from and starts refusing to tell you
where she's going.

Every generation laughs at the old
fashions, but follows religiously the new.
Henry David Thoreau

A grandpa and his grandson were playing a round of golf one afternoon. While the young man was a good golfer, his grandpa continued to offer him tips and challenges. At the eighth hole, Grandpa said, "You know, when I was your age, I could hit the ball right over the top of that tree."

So Grandson hit the ball, and it bumped the tree trunk and fell to the ground.

"Of course," Grandpa confessed, "when I was your age, that tree was only two feet tall."

## It's a generation thing if…

- You go up to the door and knock.
  They text you to let you know they're outside.

- You're doing everything to keep your hair.
  They're begging to get their head shaved.

- You cheered the day you weren't required
  to wear heels to the office.
  They're wearing 8-inch platforms.

- You offer the benefit of your wisdom
  and experience.
  They roll their eyes.

Each generation imagines itself to
be more intelligent than the one that
went before it, and wiser than the one
that comes after it.
George Orwell

When I was a boy of fourteen, my father
was so ignorant I could hardly stand to
have the old man around. But when I
got to be twenty-one, I was astonished
by how much he'd learned in seven years.
Mark Twain

GOD loves

to get

KNEE-mail.

# It's OK to Talk

Does it ever feel like no one has time for conversation anymore? You see a friend in the grocery store and step up to say hi, only to realize she's chatting into her hair. You go outdoors, greet your neighbor, but he doesn't hear you. He's got wires sticking out his ears.

By contrast—stark contrast!—there's someone whose ears are always open to you. God loves to hear the sound of your voice, and He hasn't forgotten what conversation is all about. Let all those ear buds, cellphones and headsets remind you of that.

> The LORD will hear when I call unto him.
> Psalm 4:3

When at night you cannot sleep,
talk to the Shepherd and stop
counting sheep.

If you want to talk, I'm here 24/7.
God

Prayers should be the key of the
day and the lock of the night.
Proverb

A young Sunday schooler was sent out of the classroom because of his unruly conduct. At the end of his time-out, he came back into the room and informed his teacher that he had spent the time praying about his behavior.

"Excellent," said his teacher. "If you asked God to help you make better choices, He will help you."

"Oh, that's not what I prayed for," the boy replied. "I prayed that He'd help you put up with me."

Prayer is conversation with God.
Josippon

Our prayers should be burning
words coming forth from the
furnace of a heart filled with love.
Mother Teresa

God's ear rests close to the believer's lip.

Dear God, today I haven't lost my temper, made rude remarks, repeated gossip, or gotten ticked off at anyone. I haven't taken out my frustrations on other people, refused to do kindness, or run out of patience. But I'm just about to get out of bed now, God, and from here on, I'm going to need a lot of help.

Amen

Prayer is not monologue, but dialogue.
God's voice in response to mine is its most
essential part.
Andrew Murray

The trouble with our praying is,
we just do it as a means of last resort.
Will Rogers

Prayer is nothing else than being on
terms of friendship with God.
Teresa of Avila

A woman phoned her husband at work. "I'm really sorry, honey," he told her, "but I don't have time to talk. I'm swamped with work."

She said, "This will only take a moment. I've got some good news and some bad news for you."

"Look," he said again, "I'm really busy! Just give me the good news, and please be quick about it."

"Well, here goes: The air bag works."

You're at a certain
AGE when you've
FIGURED out
the ANSWERS,
but NOBODY is asking
you QUESTIONS.

# Smart

By our age, we've been around the block, so to speak (perhaps several times). So why aren't folks paying us consultation fees just to hear our sage words of advice? Because they're too busy racing around the block, that's why.

So it's left to us to congratulate each other. Pat someone on the back, because they, too, have kicked a few curbs, gotten up, and kept on going. They, too, have turned blind corners and bumped their bean on a light post. Ouch!

We know the neighborhood, and we're here to help each other.

Encourage one another
and build each other up.
1 Thessalonians 5:11 NIV

A cleaning lady, working well beyond retirement age, was asked how she managed to keep on the job so long. "Simple," she replied. "I work for clients who can't see dust any better than I can."

What one has to do usually can be done.
Eleanor Roosevelt

As soon as you trust yourself, you will
know how to live.
Johann Wolfgang von Goethe

Nobody holds a good opinion of a man
who has a low opinion of himself.
Anthony Trollope

The president of his company who was getting on in years always scheduled staff meetings for 4:30 on Friday afternoon. One day his employees decided to ask him if staff meetings could be held on another day and at an earlier time.

"Not on your life," the savvy oldster replied. "Friday at 4:30 is the only time when I know none of you will want to disagree with me!"

# You've been around the block if you've learned…

- Not to put things away, because you'll never find them again.

- Life not only begins at 40, but it begins to show.

- Your worst enemy is gravity.

- Nothing comes free of charge, except dead batteries.

- Not to invest your money in anything that eats or needs repainting.

Endurance is not just the ability to bear
a hard thing, but to turn it into glory.
William Barclay

Experience teaches best because it gives
you individual instruction.

With the ancient is wisdom; and in length
of days understanding.
Job 12:12

I not only use all the brains that I have,
but all that I can borrow.
Woodrow Wilson

I am so clever that sometimes
I don't understand a single word
of what I am saying.
Oscar Wilde

They say that AGE
is ALL in your MIND.
The TRICK is
KEEPING it from
creeping DOWN
into your BODY.

# A Little TLC

Somewhere back in the shadows of our closet, there's a garment we just can't bear to part with. A dress, perhaps, we wore to our high school prom...the suit we donned for our first real job interview...a jacket we felt fabulous wearing. And then we decide to try it on. Big mistake.

Or not. No, you don't have the body you had at 20, but who does? But you have a body that might need a little extra TLC—because after all, it's been with you all the way from there to here.

Be renewed in the spirit of your mind.
Ephesians 4:23

Exercise daily—walk with the Lord!

How come women's magazines will
feature twelve pages of recipes,
and then follow up with twenty pages
of diet tips?

Minutes at the dinner table don't put on
weight—it's the seconds that do.

Two friends were sitting in a restaurant when one decided to order a double-fudge sundae for dessert. "You know, at our age," the other gently suggested, "we have to start counting our calories."

"Oh, I am," her dessert-craving friend replied. "I'm already at 4,892!"

A woman, concerned about her widening waist line, consulted a dietician. The dietician told her that the best way to cope with her changing metabolism was to eat regularly for two days and then skip a day. "In two weeks, you'll lose five pounds," the dietician promised.

In two weeks, the woman reported back to the dietician with the happy news that she had lost not five, but 15 pounds. "But I nearly passed out on the third day," the woman added.

"From hunger?" the dietician asked.

"No," the woman replied. "From skipping."

A middle-aged woman went to the gym and signed up for an exercise class. The receptionist told her to wear loose clothes.

"Listen," the woman protested, "if I had any loose clothes, I wouldn't be in here signing up for an exercise class!"

I'm on the BBC diet—buy bigger clothes.

Woman to weight-loss trainer: "Why would I want to get back to my original weight? I'd look ridiculous at 8 pounds, 8 ounces."

On my diet, I can't have cookies for dessert anymore, so now I have them as my appetizer.

Two kids were spending the summer with their grandparents. After a week had passed, Grandma overheard the two talking as they passed the bathroom where she kept the scales.

"Whatever you do," the elder instructed his younger sibling, "don't step on that square thing in the corner!"

"Why not?" asked sis.

"Because every time Grandma does," the boy said, "she lets out this awful loud scream!"

Middle AGE is
WHEN you're OLD
enough to KNOW
better, BUT still
YOUNG enough
to DO it.

# Bless the Day

Remember the gap between summertime and Christmas? Light years apart! But now it seems we're putting away the barbeque grill and getting out the mistletoe on the same weekend.

Maybe this is God's way of saying, "Hey! Why don't you slow down? Because, like you've discovered, time passes fast. Always has, but now you know. So why do you keep putting all the good stuff off until 'someday'?"

Today's the day to do something fun. Like untangle the twinkle lights? Nah. Something you actually want to do.

Learn to knit. Bake a pie. Go fishing.

This is the day which the LORD hath made; we will rejoice and be glad in it.
Psalm 118:24

What then is time? If no one asks me,
I know what it is. If I wish to explain
it to him who asks, I do not know.
Augustine

You can't make footprints in the sands
of time sitting down.

Dost thou love life? Then do not squander
time, for that's the stuff life is made of.
Benjamin Franklin

A state trooper saw a woman driving and knitting at the same time. He pulled up beside her, rolled down his window, and yelled, "Pull over!"

"No, officer," she shouted back, "it's a scarf!"

All of us are born gifted, but some of us
wait until later in life to open them.

To dream of the person you would like to
be is to waste the person you are.

The most important thing in our lives is
what we are doing now.

What a wonderful life I've had!
I only wish I had realized it sooner.
Colette

It is in his pleasure that a man really lives;
it is from his leisure that he constructs the
true fabric of self.
Agnes Repplier

You are younger today than you ever
will be again. Make use of it for the sake
of tomorrow.

In order to plan a vacation everyone
in the family will enjoy, what we need
is a sunny beach on the ski slopes.

The perfect lakeside campsite is where
the fish bite and the mosquitos don't.

An alternative to a vacation is to stay
home and tip every third person you see.

Time is too slow for those who wait,
too swift for those who fear,
too long for those who grieve,
too short for those who rejoice,
but for those who love,
time is eternity.

Henry van Dyke

I make the MOST
of ALL that comes
and the LEAST of
all that GOES.

*Sara Teasdale*

# All in a Day

You think your comfy outfit's just fine, but that stylish 20-something is staring at you somewhat quizzically. You find that your car regularly relocates itself on the other side of the parking lot while you shop. You mow the lawn, and feel as if it has quadrupled in area from last week.

So what's wrong with creative dressing? Or a scenic stroll through the parking lot? Or a little extra quality time with the grass?

Nothing that a little chuckle won't cut down to size.

O LORD...
the earth is full
of thy riches.
Psalm 104:24

Acceptance is going along with a smile
where you have to go anyway.

Be willing to have it so.
William James

Those who can laugh never grow old.

Mid-career, a bookkeeper decided she'd like to do something different. So she quit her job and mailed out twenty resumes with a cover letter describing her employment history and citing her strengths: accuracy, precision, and attention to detail.

Two weeks passed, and no one called to request an interview. The mystery was explained when, after three weeks, a letter arrived from one of the companies she had queried. It said, "Your resume was not enclosed as stated on your cover letter, but we want to thank you for the scrumptious brownie recipe."

Why couldn't the middle-aged woman
type on her computer for a week?
Because she had misplaced her keys.

Did you hear about the old geezer who sat
up all night wondering where the sun went?
Then it finally dawned on him.

For his 50th birthday, the kids bought their
sportsman dad a new camouflage tent.
Once he put it up, though, he could never
find it again.

Out in the Wild West, a cowboy a little past his prime sprinted from the Pony Express office, took a running leap, and landed in the middle of the road.

"What happened, pardner?" a bystander asked. "Did they throw you out of there, or are you just plain crazy?"

"They didn't throw me out, and I ain't crazy!" the cowboy growled. "I just want to find the jerk that moved my horse!"

Happiness is a function of accepting
what is.

Werner Erhard

Things turn out best for people who make
the best of the way things turn out.

Be your own best friend. Take yourself,
accept yourself, love yourself just the way
you are.

It is no use to grumble and complain;
It's just as cheap and easy to rejoice;
When God sorts out the weather
and sends rain—
Why, rain's my choice.
James Whitcomb Riley

BEAUTY always
comes from WITHIN—
within JARS,
COMPACTS, tubes
and BOTTLES.

# It's the Truth

You know the mantra, "beauty comes from within"? We say it to youngsters, and now it's time to say it to ourselves, and as many times as necessary. Physical beauty fades (and we're living proof!), but inner beauty is something we can start cultivating, and deepen, at any age.

If it takes you sitting yourself down for a heart-to-heart talk about what really counts in life…in a person…in a heart…then go ahead and do it. And then believe it, because you're telling yourself the honest truth!

Buy the truth,
and sell it not.
Proverbs 23:23

No matter how plain a woman may be,
if truth and honesty are written across her
face, she will be beautiful.

Eleanor Roosevelt

There are no better cosmetics than a
severe temperance and purity, modesty
and humility, a gracious temper and
calmness of spirit.

Arthur Helps

Though we travel the world over to find
the beautiful, we must carry it with us or
we find it not.

Ralph Waldo Emerson

BEAUTY: A six-letter word that makes people crazy. The only beauty there is, is what is on the inside. Don't make yourself feel bad if you don't like what you see. Look deeper and that is all you need. The outside is secondary, no matter what anyone says.

## It's time to cultivate inner beauty when you look in the mirror and…

- Realize that your worst enemy is gravity.

- Discover the hair you used to have on your head now lodges in your nose and ears.

- Notice a striking similarity between your actual face and the photo in your passport.

- Find that your skin doesn't fit as well as it used to.

- Decide to forego organic foods, because you need all the preservatives you can get.

- Use caulking compound to camouflage the circles under your eyes.

In a crowded motor vehicle bureau, a woman was waiting for her license to be printed. When her name was called, she went over and picked up the first card she saw. "Eeeew!" she exclaimed, "I can't believe I look that old and decrepit!"

And red in the face, too, when the woman behind her said, "That's mine!" and snatched the card from her hand.

As one old toad croaked to the other,
"Love you lots...warts and all."

SOME folks
are WISE
and SOME are
OTHERWISE.

*Tobias Smollett*

# Wise Guys

Wisdom doesn't always come along with gray hair, but it's a nice thought. That's not to say it can't or won't, but just it's not contained in hair follicles.

Defining wisdom, of course, is like trying to grab hold of soft gelatin. Its meaning slips around when we try to grasp it with words like savvy, serene, spiritual, deep thinking…but we know it when we see it.

Though wisdom doesn't come with gray hair, it takes time to develop it and nurture it, and maturity to treasure it, which is a very wise thing to do at any age.

The price of wisdom
is above rubies.
Job 28:18

Be happy. It's one way of being wise.

Colette

The years teach much which the days
never knew.

Ralph Waldo Emerson

Common sense in an uncommon degree
is what the world calls wisdom.

Samuel Taylor Coleridge

The final in a philosophy class consisted of a one-question exam. The professor picked up a chair, plopped it atop his desk, and wrote on the board: "Using everything we have learned this semester, prove to me that this chair does not exist."

Students, with furrowed brows, began to write furiously. One student, however, finished in under a minute, turned in his paper, and left the classroom.

When the grades were posted, his was the only A. His astonished classmates asked to see his exam paper. On it he had written: "What chair?"

## Words of wisdom for the wise...

- We're only young once, but we can remain immature forever.

- Despite all the new and improved headache relievers, there are still headaches.

- Always go the extra mile, especially if what you're after is a mile away.

- Brain cells come and brain cells go, but fat cells stay with you forever.

- The colder the X-ray machine, the more of your body you will be asked to put on it.

- Be true to your teeth, or they will be false to you.

- Never lie to CAT Scan technicians, because they can see right through you.

- Don't be old until you have lived.

The art of being wise is the art of knowing what to overlook.

William James

The young man knows the rules, but the old man knows the exceptions.

Oliver Wendell Holmes, Sr.

Wisdom is the sunlight of the soul.

Proverb

A man should never be ashamed to own that he has been in the wrong, which is but saying, in other words, that he is wiser today than he was yesterday.

Jonathan Swift

# GRATITUDE
## is the HEART'S MEMORY.

*Proverb*

# Going Forward

Gray, silver, salt-and-pepper—call it what you will. We know what you're talking about. There are also the little thin lines settling in to stay. The upper arms that aren't quite as firm as they used to be.

Unlike your car, you don't come with a reverse gear. So all you can do is go forward with a smile—and gratitude. Gratitude for the many good times you've had, for the tough times you've come through, and for the gift of today.

Gratitude is a grand traveling companion wherever you are on the road of life.

In every thing give thanks.
1 Thessalonians 5:18

If the only prayer you said in your whole life was, "thank you," that would suffice.
Meister Eckhart

Gratitude is the best attitude.

If you can't be thankful for what you have received, at least be thankful for what you have escaped.

A friend, trying to cheer up a cranky oldster, suggested he might try being thankful for his blessings.

"Me?" he sniffed. "What have I got to be thankful for? I can't even pay my bills!"

The friend said, "Well, you can be very thankful indeed that you aren't one of your creditors."

Wise people count their blessings;
fools count their problems.

When you drink from a stream,
remember the source.
Proverb

Seeds of discouragement will not
grow in a thankful heart.

At dinner, Dad invited his young son to say a table prayer. The boy bowed his head and thanked God for the fried chicken, the mashed potatoes, and the brownies that were to come for dessert.

Then he looked up at his dad and asked, "If I thank God for the Brussels sprouts, will He know I'm lying?"

## Be thankful that…

- Wrinkles don't hurt.

- Graying hair doesn't make you gain weight.

- You don't always catch everything everyone says… or feel you need to.

For each new morning with its light,
For rest and shelter of the night,
For health and food, for love and friends,
For everything Thy goodness sends.
Ralph Waldo Emerson

Every TOMORROW
has TWO handles.
We can TAKE HOLD
of it by the HANDLE
of ANXIETY, or by the
HANDLE of FAITH.

*Henry Ward Beecher*